S0-ACU-717

The Box Jellyfish

Laura L. Sullivan

3 9082 13145 2917

Published in 2018 by Cavendish Square Publishing, LLC
243 5th Avenue, Suite 136, New York, NY 10016

Library of Congress Cataloging-in-Publication Data

Names: Sullivan, Laura L., 1974- , author.
Title: The box jellyfish / Laura L. Sullivan.
Description: New York : Cavendish Square Publishing, 2018. | Series: Toxic creatures | Includes index.
Identifiers: LCCN 2016048788 (print) | LCCN 2016054775 (ebook) | ISBN 9781502625991 (pbk.) |
ISBN 9781502625793 (6 pack) | ISBN 9781502625939 (library bound) | ISBN 9781502625861 (E-book)
Subjects: LCSH: Cubomedusae--Juvenile literature.
Classification: LCC QL377.S4 S85 2017 (print) | LCC QL377.S4 (ebook) | DDC 593.5/3--dc23
LC record available at https://lccn.loc.gov/2016048788

Editorial Director: David McNamara
Editor: Fletcher Doyle
Copy Editor: Nathan Heidelberger
Associate Art Director: Amy Greenan
Designer: Alan Sliwinski
Production Coordinator: Karol Szymczuk
Photo Research: J8 Media

The photographs in this book are used by permission and through the courtesy of: Cover, 15 Paul Sutherland/
National Geographic/Getty Images; throughout book, Deliverance/Shutterstock.com; p. 4 Melanie
Stetson Freeman/Christian Science Monitor/Getty Images; p. 6 KGrif/Shutterstock.com; p. 7 Wikimedia
Commons/Jan Bielecki, Alexander K. Zaharoff, Nicole Y. Leung, Anders Garm, Todd H. Oakley (edited by
Ruthven (talk))/File:Tripedalia-cystophora.png/CC SA 4.0; p. 8 Nature Picture Library/Alamy Stock Photo;
p. 9 Aekikuis/Shutterstock.com; p. 11 Dikobraziy/Shutterstock.com; p. 13 PeteKaras/Shutterstock.com;
p. 14 Wikimedia Commons/Spaully at English Wikipedia/File:Nematocyst discharge.png/CC SA 1.0; p. 16
DonyaHH/Shutterstock.com; p. 17 Jake Nowakowski/Newspix/Getty Images; p. 18, 22, 25 Auscape/UIG/
Getty Images; p. 19 Wikimedia Commons/Anynobody/File:Irukandjijellyfishsize.png/CC SA 3.0; p. 20 Anthony
Behar/Sipa/AP Images; p. 24 Roger Horrocks/Gallo Images/Getty Images; p. 26 Wikimedia Commons/
Colin Henein/File:JellyfishNetAustralia.JPG/CC SA 3.0; p. 27 Lawrence Bartlett/AFP/Getty Images.

Printed in the United States of America

CONTENTS

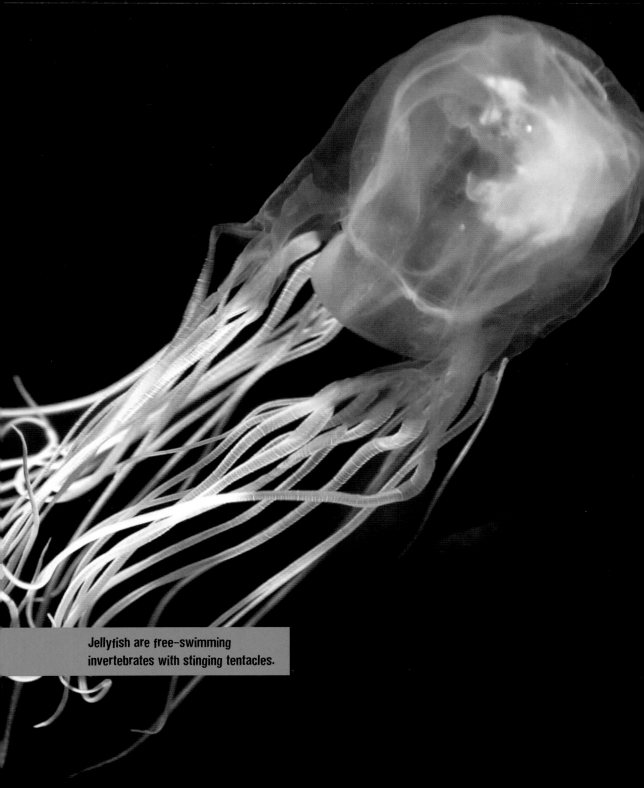

Jellyfish are free-swimming invertebrates with stinging tentacles.

Advanced Jellyfish

Box jellyfish are a type of marine animal. They are known for their cube-shaped bodies and their deadly stings. Some species of box jellyfish are only mildly toxic. Others can stop an adult human's heart within a few minutes.

Jellyfish are invertebrates. This means they do not have a backbone. Their bodies are called the bell. Tentacles hang under the bell. Jellyfish **evolved** at least five hundred million years ago. There are

Jellyfish are related to sea anemones. You can see some similarities in their bodies.

jellyfish in salt water and freshwater. Most are in salt water. They are related to sea anemones and corals.

Box jellies are named for their cube-shaped bodies. One or several tentacles hang from each of the four corners. In the center of the bell, on the underside, is a shape like a hose. It has a mouth on the end of it.

Box jellyfish are among the most advanced jellies. All jellyfish move with the currents of the water. They also move by taking water into their bell and then squeezing the bell. This is called **pulsing**. Box jellies have a bell that makes extra force when it pulses. They can move very fast for a jellyfish. They can swim as fast as 4.6 miles per hour (7.4 kilometers per hour).

Box jellyfish have sophisticated eyes, unlike most species of jellyfish.

Most jellyfish have poor eyesight. They can only tell light from dark or see rough movement or shapes. But box jellies have complex eyes. They have four eyes with lenses, **corneas**, and **retinas**, just like more advanced creatures. They also have twenty simple eyes that just see light and dark.

Most jellyfish can only drift with the current. They rely on luck to snag a meal. Box jellies use their speed to chase food. They can see their prey and go after

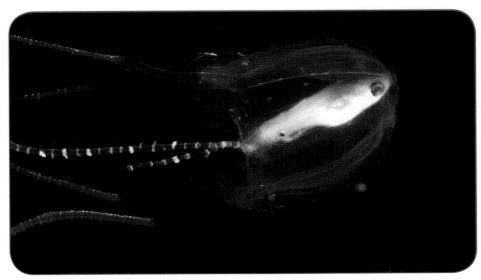

Box jellyfish can actively hunt their prey.

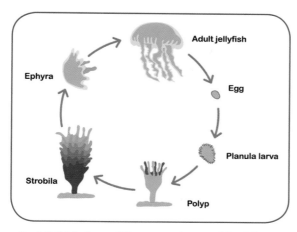

Box jellyfish look very different at each stage of their life cycle.

Adult jellyfish

Ephyra

Egg

Planula larva

Strobila

Polyp

it. They can also avoid predators. Despite the fierce stinging tentacles, several kinds of fish and sea turtles eat box jellyfish.

Box jellyfish are either male or female. However, each one is able to make both eggs and sperm. They release the eggs and sperm into the water. These join to make **larvae** that swim. The larvae develop into **polyps.** A polyp is shaped like a tube. It sticks to a hard surface on one end. It has a mouth and tentacles at the other end. These polyps form buds that grow into other polyps. Each polyp makes several disks that turn into the bells of adult jellyfish.

Box Jellyfish Quick Facts

Name: Box jellies are named for the square shape of their bell. Their class name, Cubozoa, also refers to their cube-like shape. There are five species of the most toxic box jellies, the Irukandji. Irukandji jellies were named after the Aboriginal people who live on the coast of Queensland, Australia. They traveled on the sea. **Aborigines** are people who have lived in a place from the earliest times.

Range: Box jellyfish can be found worldwide in warm tropical and subtropical oceans. The most dangerous species are mostly found in the Indo-Pacific region. These are the tropical parts of the Indian Ocean and the west-central Pacific Ocean.

Size: The largest box jellyfish can be 12 inches (30 centimeters) across the top of the bell, with tentacles stretching nearly 10 feet (3 meters). The smallest are less than 0.5 inches (1.3 cm), with tentacles just a few inches long.

Species: There are thirty-six species of box jellyfish.

Fun Fact: While most jellies sting only with their tentacles, the Irukandji box jellies have stingers on their bells, too.

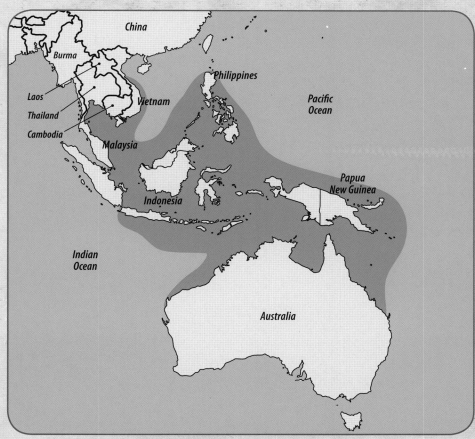

Box jellyfish can be found worldwide, but they are most common in the tropical Indo-Pacific waters and around Australia (shown in green).

Box jellyfish are dangerous enough to need warning signs.

Dangerous Dart

Often, people call any harmful substance "poison." However, the terms "poisonous," "toxic," and "venomous" are not the same.

A toxin is a harmful substance made by animals, plants, or other organisms. A toxic substance is poisonous if it causes harm when it is ingested (eaten) or when it enters the body through the skin or lungs. Venom is a toxin that is put in the body by a fang, barb, or stinger. When a venom is swallowed,

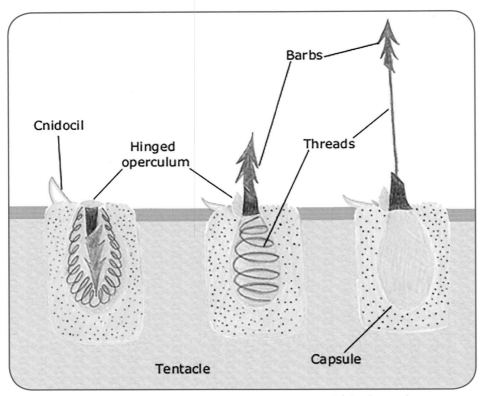

Box jellyfish nematocysts fire and inject venom when they touch fish or human skin.

stomach acids destroy it. Box jellyfish are venomous because they inject their toxins.

The stinging cells of a box jellyfish's tentacles are called **nematocysts**. Each tiny nematocyst cell has a dart inside. There are thousands of nematocysts on each tentacle. When the nematocysts come in contact with skin, they fire, injecting many tiny darts loaded with venom.

The most dangerous box jellyfish is the large sea wasp. People say its sting feels like having red-hot metal pressed against the skin. The pain is not the worst problem. The venom makes the body's cells leak potassium. This leads to rapid heart failure. Death can occur within two to five minutes. The

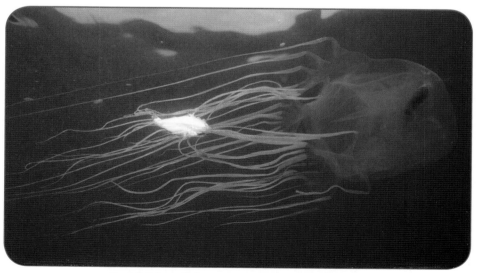

Box jellyfish use their venomous tentacles to stun their prey.

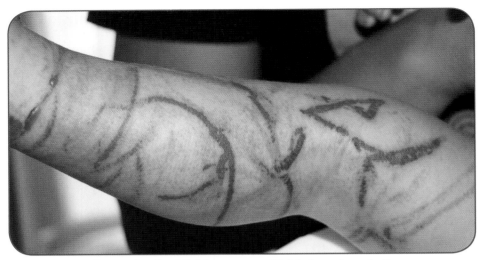
Most species of box jellyfish can cause terrible injuries, and even death.

effects happen so fast that many victims can't make it back to shore before they die. If the heart stops, **CPR** must be started right away. There is an **antivenom** to some box jellyfish stings. Some symptoms harm victims before they can be treated.

The tiny Irukandji jellies can also kill. Their venom is one hundred times more powerful than a cobra's. And it is one thousand times stronger than a tarantula's. Their sting may cause Irukandji syndrome.

The little Irukandji jelly is less than 0.5 inches (1.3 cm) long, but it can be deadly.

Because they are so small, their sting isn't usually very painful right away. People say it feels like a bee sting, or even a mosquito bite. Some people don't even know they've been stung. About thirty minutes later, painful, scary symptoms start. These symptoms include headache, bad pain in the back and abdomen, vomiting, sweating, high blood pressure, and rapid pulse. The venom even affects the mind. Victims get feelings of doom. They are often so sure

A Bad Hand

One of the largest box jellies is the sea wasp, also called *Chironex fleckeri*. It was discovered by, and named after, Dr. Hugo Flecker in 1955. After a five-year-old Australian boy was killed by an unknown jellyfish near Cairns, Dr. Flecker captured several species of jellies in the area. That's when he found this new and very deadly species. The genus name *Chironex* means "murdering hand."

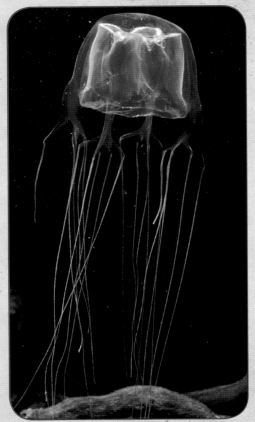

The sea wasp is among the largest of the box jellyfish.

The Irukandji jellyfish has a tiny bell but can have long tentacles.

they will die that they've begged doctors to kill them. They want to get it over with. The symptoms usually last from a few hours to a day, but may linger for weeks.

To treat a box jelly sting—or any jellyfish sting— first clean it with a lot of vinegar. Vinegar stops the nematocysts from firing. Next, get rid of any stingers. Rubbing them with a towel may cause them to keep firing. They should be pulled off with tweezers, or shaved off with a blade or a credit card.

The sea wasp has killed at least sixty-four people in Australia since 1883. That was the first year records were kept. It has killed even more people in nearby countries. The antivenom and medical care are not as available in these places. Children are more likely

Distance swimmers wear many kinds of protection, including prosthetic face masks, to avoid jellyfish stings. This mask was worn by Diana Nyad.

to die when stung due to their size. Though box jellyfish are most common around Australia and Indonesia, some species live off US coasts. A four-year-old boy was killed by a box jelly off Galveston Island, Texas, in 1990. Irukandji have been found off the Florida coast. Several military combat divers working around Key West have had what appears to be Irukandji syndrome.

Scientists can learn a lot from the
venomous box jellyfish—if they are careful.

CHAPTER THREE

Removing the Sting

Scientists are still learning about what makes jellyfish venom so deadly. They try to separate the useful parts of the venom from the ones that cause deadly side effects. They also need to study the venom to make more effective antivenoms. An antivenom exists for one kind of box jelly, but not for all of them.

Harvesting some kinds of venom is easy. To get snake venom, a researcher will carefully hold the snake and get it to bite through a membrane over a bottle. The venom will drip down. Then it can be studied. Getting jellyfish venom was much harder. However, scientists recently discovered a way to do it. Ethanol (alcohol) will force the nematocysts to fire. (This is why alcohol should never be used to treat jellyfish stings!) Then they can collect the venom for study.

In certain conditions, masses of box jellies can be found near shore, endangering swimmers.

Swimmers should take warnings of box jellyfish very seriously.

In places like Australia with a lot of box jellyfish, and a lot of swimming tourists, people are always looking for ways to avoid stings. Many beaches enclose swimming areas with nets during jellyfish season. This keeps out most jellyfish. Some jellyfish seem to avoid the color red, so some of the nets are made with red material.

Covering your skin with pantyhose can prevent stings. People have known this for a long time. However, they did not know the reason why. At first, people thought the hose was just thick enough to keep the nematocysts from touching the skin. Later, it was learned that nematocysts don't fire

Many Australian beaches have enclosed areas with nets to protect swimmers from deadly box jellyfish.

In some areas where box jellies are common, there are vinegar stations to flush the wounds.

every time they touch something. The stinging cells are triggered by chemicals on the skin, whether of a human or a fish. When the tentacles touch the pantyhose, they don't detect the right chemicals, so they don't fire.

Toxic Creatures Quiz

1. In what ways are box jellyfish more advanced than many other kinds of jellyfish?

2. What tiny kind of box jellies can cause symptoms like headache, bad pain in the back and abdomen, vomiting, sweating, high blood pressure, rapid pulse, and feelings of doom?

3. How quickly can the box jellyfish known as a sea wasp kill a human?

4. Why should you never use alcohol on jellyfish stings?

GLOSSARY

Aborigine One of the original inhabitants of Australia.

antivenom A substance given to fight the effects of venom.

cornea The clear covering of the eyeball that lets in light.

CPR Cardiopulmonary resuscitation, a medical procedure to keep blood flowing through the body after the heart stops beating.

evolve To change slowly into a state that is more advanced.

larva The young form of a jellyfish that is free swimming, before it becomes a polyp.

nematocyst The stinging cell on a jellyfish tentacle.

polyp The stage of a jellyfish life cycle that attaches to rocks.

pulsing A regular widening of the bell of a jellyfish to take in and eject water to provide movement.

retina Sensitive tissue at the back of the eye that gets images and signals the brain about what has been seen.

FIND OUT MORE

Books

Gowell, Elizabeth. *Amazing Jellies*. Piermont, NH: Bunker Hill Publishing, 2004.

Spilsbury, Louise. *Jellyfish*. A Day in the Life: Sea Animals. Portsmouth, NH: Heinemann, 2010.

Websites

National Geographic: Box Jellyfish

http://animals.nationalgeographic.com/animals/invertebrates/box-jellyfish

This site not only has information about box jellyfish but also provides an array of photos of the beautiful but deadly creatures.

NOAA: What Is the Most Dangerous Marine Animal?

http://oceanservice.noaa.gov/facts/box-jellyfish.html

The National Oceanic and Atmospheric Administration answers the question: What is the most dangerous animal in the ocean?

INDEX

Page numbers in **boldface** are illustrations. Entries in **boldface** are glossary terms.

ABOUT THE AUTHOR

Laura L. Sullivan is the author of more than forty fiction and nonfiction books for children, including the fantasies *Under the Green Hill* and *Guardian of the Green Hill*. She has written many books for Cavendish Square, including four titles in the Toxic Creatures series.